Original title:
The Shores of Serenity

Copyright © 2025 Creative Arts Management OÜ
All rights reserved.

Author: Ryan Sterling
ISBN HARDBACK: 978-1-80581-531-0
ISBN PAPERBACK: 978-1-80581-058-2
ISBN EBOOK: 978-1-80581-531-0

Serenity's Gentle Kiss

A seagull steals my sandwich, what a trick,
Waves laughing hard, with a gentle flick.
The sun is a warm hug, but a bit too bold,
It leaves me baked like a loaf of bread, I'm told.

Sand between my toes, it's quite the treat,
But grains in my sandwich? That's no way to eat!
A child building castles, the tide takes their throne,
'That's not a palace!' I heard them moan.

Embracing the Calm Waters

Floating on a raft, I'm a champion of chill,
Paddleboarders zooming by, they've got some skill.
My sunscreen's a beacon, I'm sure it attracts,
Fish swim by, thinking I'm a human snack!

Beach balls fly and cars honk with glee,
Trying to catch a wave? That's just not me.
I drink my coconut and let out a sigh,
Befriending a crab that just scuttled by.

Murmurs of the Gentle Shore

Whispers from the shells, they gossip quite loud,
Sharing secrets of fish, and tales of the crowd.
A tall tale of mermaids with glittery fins,
They say they hold parties and serve salty sins!

Children chase seagulls, thinking they'll win,
When all they get back is a smirk and a spin.
I join in the fun, I've got nothing to hide,
Laughing 'til my sunscreen begins to slide!

Tide Pools of Reflection

Tide pools glimmer, but oh what a tease,
A crab waves hello, but swims with such ease.
I ponder each splash, it's hard not to smile,
Like trying to catch laughter, it may take a while.

Starfish strike a pose, in the world's smallest dance,
While clam shells pretend to give life a chance.
I trip on a rock, then laugh at my plight,
Nature watches closely, enjoying my light.

Beyond the Ebb and Flow

Waves giggle as they race,
Wandering gulls make a fuss.
Crabs wear hats made of shells,
Laughing at the trains of bus.

Seagulls drop fries from their beaks,
Fish wave back with a splash.
Turtles slow dance in circles,
They even have a mustache!

The tide comes in for a chat,
It winks at the sandy shore.
While the sun just sits and grins,
As if it's seen this dance before.

Shells collect stories untold,
Whispers of the ocean's jest.
With each wave a new joke unfolds,
Making the beach a comedy fest.

Ribbon of Dreams by the Sea

The tide brings forth ribbons of foam,
   Mermaids knit while sipping tea.
   Jellyfish float by like balloons,
     Singing tunes of mystery.

Seashells swap tales under the moon,
   Crabs play cards on the sand.
   A dolphin pipes up with a joke,
     And all the fish just stand.

Seagulls strut like they own the place,
   Wiggling their toes in delight.
   A starfish tries to start a dance,
   Laughing until the morning light.

Each wave is a punchline waiting to roll,
   As laughter bubbles up in glee.
   A tapestry woven with joy and play,
     A life bright and full by the sea.

Odes to the Solitary Cove

The cove wears a cloak of tranquility,
But whispers of mischief abound.
A crab takes a selfie at dawn,
As tourists wander around.

Seals play peek-a-boo with the sun,
While the pelicans giggle in flight.
The rocks are entertained by their pranks,
A cheerful, quirky sight.

Fish don their best outfits for show,
As waves cheer them, 'Hip, hip, hooray!'
The seaweed sways like it's grooving,
Creating a splash on display.

So come join the laughter and fun,
In a cove where smiles are free.
Each moment is filled with pure glee,
A joyous life by the sea.

Sanctuary Beneath the Stars

Underneath the twinkling light,
Crabs recite their best jokes.
Stars giggle, lighting up the night,
As the ocean gently strokes.

Whales tell tales of long-lost ships,
While minnows practice their dance.
The moon joins in, humming tunes,
And crabs seize every chance.

Seashells echo laughter around,
As waves play tag with the shore.
A playful breeze swoops down to chat,
While the cosmos roars with rapport.

In this haven where joy takes flight,
Where chuckles echo galore.
Join the blithe spirit of the night,
And let laughter be your oar.

Melodies of Peaceful Tides

Seaweed dances to the sound,
A crab's little pinch astounds.
Waves hum a quirky tune,
As seagulls wear their hats at noon.

Fishermen tell tales so grand,
About the fish that got away, unplanned.
Mermaids giggle with delight,
In the glow of the moonlit night.

Sunburned tourists lose their way,
While flip-flops take the lead today.
An octopus plays chess with a clam,
In a beachside, sun-drenched jam.

Sandcastles teeter, then collapse,
While children run with giggling flaps.
At every splash, a wave of cheer,
The ocean whispers, "No need to fear!"

Reflections Beneath the Endless Sky

The sun wears shades upon its face,
As clouds play hide and seek with grace.
Dolphins leap in a silly dance,
With winks and flips, they take a chance.

A floating buoy sings a tune,
While fishermen hum the same monsoon.
Seashells gossip on the shore,
About the tides and plans galore.

Windy kites laugh in the breeze,
As a gull steals fries with such ease.
Sunsets drape in colors so bright,
While starfish giggle at the sight.

Reflections shimmer like jokes untold,
The ocean's humor, a sight to behold.
With every splash, a joke unfolds,
At night, the waves will sing of gold.

Gentle Currents of Calm

Waves roll in like a soft embrace,
Pine trees sway in a graceful race.
Sand between toes feels like delight,
While ants march on in a quirky flight.

Frogs serenade with croaks so loud,
As kids build shrimp stands, feeling proud.
The breeze whispers secrets and schemes,
While dolphins plot their silly dreams.

A picnic basket flies quite high,
When a seagull swoops from the sky.
Beach balls bounce with a happy thrill,
As laughter echoes on the hill.

The horizon wears a silly grin,
As waves play tag without a fin.
To the rhythm of the calming tide,
Comes a humor we cannot hide.

Embrace of the Restful Horizon

Sunset snacks with a raisin toast,
Seagulls serving as the ghost host.
Lazy waves coax at your feet,
In this paradise, life feels sweet.

The horizon yawns, stretching wide,
While rubber ducks take a wild ride.
Underneath the laughing sun,
Fish wear hats, having some fun.

Lemonade spills as friends chuckle,
As crabs initiate the dance shuffle.
The ocean refers to a library of laughs,
Where seaweed tells of its silly paths.

As day bids adieu with a chuckle and wink,
The stars begin their cosmic sync.
In this embrace, joy finds a way,
To turn every frown into play.

The Calm Between the Storms

In a boat made of tuna cans,
We sailed past jellyfish bands.
The clouds wore a funny hat,
While the waves danced like a chubby cat.

Seagulls squawked jokes on the breeze,
While fish laughed beneath the seas.
We tossed our worries to the gull,
And laughed as the tide began to lull.

Lullabies from the Ocean Floor

The starfish sing in off-key tunes,
While crabs play maracas with spoons.
A clam joined in, trying to hum,
But ended up sounding quite dumb.

The seaweed swayed to a silly rhyme,
While dolphins perfected their slapstick mime.
The ocean giggled, waves did clap,
As the sandcastle kings took a nap.

Footprints in the Softest Sand

Footprints were made by a dancing toe,
And a crab who thought he could steal the show.
Seagulls reenacted a drama so neat,
As a toddler lost his ice cream treat.

Waves tickled ankles in playful delight,
While shells whispered secrets all through the night.
The sun threw its rays, dressed in bright hues,
Reflecting on all the silly old views.

A Symphony of Sea and Sky

The clouds decided to form a band,
While the ocean played marbles with the sand.
The waves trumpeted with all their might,
As the sun waggled its rays, oh what a sight!

A pelican requested a funny song,
And starfish joined in, singing along.
With laughter filling the salty air,
Nothing felt better than this sandy affair.

Tranquility's Embrace

On sandy beaches, crabs do dance,
While seagulls steal your lunch by chance.
The waves throw jokes, they splash and play,
As beach balls float and slip away.

Lifeguards snooze in their high seats,
While sunbathers roast like barbecue meats.
Flip-flops squeak, and laughter roams,
Nature calls, but so do phones!

Ice cream drips, it's a sticky fight,
Seagulls plot; it's quite the sight.
Sunburned noses tell tales in red,
Of fun in sun, and laughs, widespread.

But as we leave, our hearts will soar,
For there's always room for one joke more.
In this paradise where laughter meets,
Joyful memories mix with sandy treats.

The Color of Serenity

Blue as the sky and green as grass,
We paint this place with all our sass.
Even the beach umbrellas fight,
For mischief hides in colors bright.

The sunset blushes in shades of fun,
While waves tickle toes, on the run.
Sandy dogs chase after the tide,
With silly leaps that can't be denied.

Fishermen tell tales that grow with the bait,
As fish play tricks, oh, isn't that great?
Towels spread like altars of joy,
Where sunscreen battles a sneaky boy.

The ocean hums a lullaby tune,
Under the watchful, winking moon.
Colorful memories, layered with glee,
In this vibrant place, wild and free.

Dance of the Celestial Ocean

The stars in the sky begin a jig,
While dolphins dive and do a gig.
Moonbeams sparkle like disco lights,
As waves shimmy through magical nights.

Crabs in tuxedos strut on the shore,
Each step they take, they ask for more.
The conch shells hum a melodic tune,
While jellyfish glide like balloons.

Tides swipe left, and tides swipe right,
Seats chosen by an expert knight.
The ocean's rhythm plays all day,
In this grand, aquatic cabaret.

With belly laughs and splashes loud,
We're dancing now, and feeling proud.
In this celestial waltz, hearts glow,
Where waves invite all to join the show.

Driftwood Dreams

A log drifts by, with a grin so wide,
It dreams of travels, a silly ride.
A starfish yells, 'Let's build a boat!'
While waves respond with a playful gloat.

Pelicans ponder, shall we soar?
Or play a game of beach ball lore?
As driftwood schemes, they plot and plan,
In this sandy kingdom, they're the clan.

Naptime comes, but jokes don't cease,
Seashells whisper secrets of bliss.
Waves' ticklish touch, can't help but tease,
As floating dreams settle with ease.

With every tide, fresh laughter flows,
A driftwood family, as friendship grows.
In the sun's embrace, we come to rest,
Where dreams drift by, and life's the best.

Calm Beyond the Riptide

Waves dance like they're at a ball,
Crabs cutting rug and having a ball.
Seagulls squawk with witty remarks,
While sunbathers nap and miss all the sparks.

Flip-flops flung, a wild chase in sight,
Kids squeal loud, oh what a delight!
Beach balls sail like they've got flair,
While sunscreen fights to tame back the glare.

Sandcastles rise, then plop with a sound,
As a jet ski zooms by, splashing around.
Laughter erupts with each hullabaloo,
Ocean's mischief is just too good to rue.

So grab a drink, let's toast to the tide,
Where goofy antics and joys collide.
The sea may churn, but here it's a joke,
In happy chaos, our hearts just poke.

Melodies from the Coastal Wind

Gentle breezes hum a soft tune,
Bringing giggles like a cartoon.
Kites hover high in the vibrant blue,
With tails like ribbons, a colorful crew.

Turtles race, no time to lose,
While surfers negotiate their moves.
Seashells whisper secrets they keep,
As dolphins bounce, oh, what a leap!

A picnic spread, with snacks galore,
Ants march in line, asking for more.
Soda cans pop, a fizzy cheer,
As laughter rolls, it's clear we're near.

Wrapped in sunshine, our spirits lift,
With goofy jokes, that's the real gift.
The coastal breeze carries joy anew,
Serene fun awaits, just me and you.

Emotions Woven in Salt and Sand

The sun's a puppet with a bright string,
It pulls at our hearts, makes them swing.
A starfish winks, how could we miss?
On this sandy stage, it's pure bliss.

Flip-flops flapping, a comical scare,
As beach balls bounce without a care.
Towels misplaced, a sunburnt prize,
We laugh as we watch our friends' surprise.

Ice cream drips, a sweet cascade,
From sticky fingers, laughter's made.
Seagulls dive-bombing our tasty treats,
While kids run circles—tiny, swift feats.

In this warm haze, our hearts do sing,
As we do our best to avoid the sting.
With salty smiles, we embrace the groove,
The shoreline of fun, it's our favorite move.

Breaths of Peace at the Water's Edge

A surfboard's waiting, can't wait to ride,
With more spills and thrills, it's hard to hide.
Watermelon fights in the sunshine beam,
What a delightful, splashy dream!

Mermaids giggle in the foamy flow,
Every wave brings a new show.
Squirt guns blazing, oh what a scene,
Dripping laughter fits right in between.

Beach towels spread, a feast so grand,
Sandy sandwiches crafted by hand.
As we munch and crunch, the seagulls squawk,
Impersonating a funny folk talk.

At twilight's blush, our toes in the sand,
We share silly stories, magic unplanned.
In every chuckle, a spark of glee,
Peace finds us here, where we're totally free.

Whispers of the Tidal Breeze

The ocean calls with a silly tune,
Seagulls dance under the sun of June.
Waves giggle as they crash on shore,
Finding sandcastles, they leave wanting more.

Crabs don their hats, feigning a stroll,
Shells play poker, chips and a roll.
A fish with a mustache flips in delight,
As jellyfish juggle, what a funny sight.

Beach towels flutter like flags in the breeze,
While kids chase after mischievous fleas.
The tide whispers secrets to sandy toes,
With laughs from the shore, anything goes!

So grab your flip-flops, come join the fun,
The laughter here echoes, second to none.
For in this realm where the ocean plays,
Every moment sparkles, brightening days.

Tranquil Reflections at Dusk

As daylight fades in a peachy swirl,
Waves yawn softly, their tails unfurl.
A crab reads a book upside down,
While starfish practice their best frown.

Seashells gossip, sharing the tide,
Chasing little fish with nowhere to hide.
A dolphin's laugh echoes in the night,
As fireflies join in, glowing so bright.

Balloons drift by, tied to seaweed,
While mermaids mingle and dance with speed.
The moon winks down, casting silver beams,
Tickling the waves, oh, if only dreams!

With waves of laughter, the ocean glows,
Each ripple a giggle, as the sunset flows.
In this peaceful blend, no worries to find,
Just silliness here, to lighten the mind.

Beneath the Gentle Waves

Beneath the surface, a fish wears a crown,
While sea cucumbers dance, upside down.
A clam's got a joke, it's hard to believe,
As coral reefs giggle, never to grieve.

An octopus tickles with its many arms,
Chasing shy shrimp, with all of its charms.
The seaweed sways, caught in a trance,
As turtles in shades join the underwater dance.

Fish-flavored chips, a snack in the brine,
An iguana sits sipping on seaweed wine.
Crabs play hide-and-seek, giggling they scurry,
While sea otters hold paws, never in a hurry.

So let's dive deep into oceanic cheer,
Where every creature has a joke to share.
For beneath these waves, a funny brigade,
Awaits our laughter, never to fade.

Harmony in the Ocean's Embrace

The tides jive and shake in a bubbly whirl,
As starfish strut, giving barnacles a twirl.
Seagulls crack jokes, their humor quite dry,
While dolphins splash high, reaching for the sky.

A walrus wears glasses, reading the news,
While clowns in the coral exchange their views.
The rhythm of waves tap dances along,
Every splash and giggle creating a song.

Anemones sway, conducting the show,
With a crab as a drummer, putting on a glow.
The sunset giggles, painting the sea,
As fish in tuxedos sip on iced tea.

So join in the laughter, there's plenty to share,
With nature's sweet humor hanging in the air.
For in this embrace of the ocean-wide,
Every wave brings joy, each tide a joyride.

In the Arms of Oceanic Peace

Seashells gossip, oh how they chat,
Under a wave, there's a party, quite fat.
Dancing with seaweed, a silly affair,
Crabs on a conga line, filled with flair.

Seagulls are comedians, swooping with grace,
Stealing my sandwich, they run the rat race.
Fish wear tiny glasses, looking so sly,
Telling tall tales as they swim by.

Sandcastles crumble, they shout, "We're done!"
A sand dollar governor, having some fun.
Tiny beach bums with their toys in tow,
Building a kingdom, all in a row.

So here I sit, in pure blissful glee,
While the shells whisper jokes, just for me.
With laughter, I float on a soft ocean breeze,
No worries, just joy, oh, what a tease!

Dreamscapes at Water's Edge

The tide rolls in with a giggle so bright,
Tickling my toes, in the morning light.
A dolphin with shades glides right overhead,
While flip-flops are flying, oh where are they led?

Little crabs shuffle, they've got their own dance,
To a tune played by seagulls, what a chance!
Starfish gathered 'round, with a starry-eyed look,
Plotting a drama straight out of a book.

The sun paints the sky in a silly hue,
While I chase coconut flies, the mischief they do.
A jellyfish winks, sporting a sash,
In this wild wonderland, time seems to dash.

As waves play hopscotch, I laugh with delight,
Every splash around me feels perfectly right.
In dreams by the water, oh how we conspire,
To enjoy every moment, our hearts set on fire!

A Sojourn in the Gentle Currents

Waves flirt with toes, what a cheeky affair,
Mermaids chuckle, tossing their hair.
A turtle in shades takes a break from the race,
While I sip my drink, feeling quite out of place.

Bubbles are popping, like fireworks on cue,
My floaty's a throne, with a magnificent view.
Crabs march in formation, all in a row,
Chanting their anthem: "To the sea, let's go!"

The clouds turn to marshmallows, soft as a dream,
While the wind sings a tune, like a sweet ice cream.
A pelican chuckles, looking quite smart,
"Why fly when you can just grace the art?"

As laughter ripples through this watery land,
I paddle along, never making a plan.
In gentle currents, mistakes turn to cheer,
Adventure awaits, so let's spread some beer!

Starry Skies Above the Waves

Stars twinkle down, like a sparkly show,
While fish in tuxedos swim to and fro.
The moon pulls a prank, causing waves to dance,
As night creatures shimmer, all in a trance.

A glow-in-the-dark octopus joins the fun,
With disco ball vibes, everyone's spun.
Splashing and laughing, they create quite a scene,
While I try to join in, pretending to glean.

Constellations giggle in their bedazzled attire,
As comets race by, oh, they never tire.
I swear I saw Neptune just laughing so free,
As sea turtles boogie, inviting me.

So here beneath starlight, with magic so near,
The ocean's a playground, and I'm full of cheer.
As the tides tell stories, both silly and grand,
I float through the night, with joy, hand in hand!

Sheltered by the Whispering Waves

Seagulls squawk while I sip my tea,
The waves giggle, just wait and see.
A crab sidesteps with a clumsy flair,
While the sun plays peekaboo in the air.

Flip-flops flying, a beach ball spree,
Kids' laughter is wild, as wild can be.
I trip on sand, oh what a sight!
Dancing with waves, they just feel right.

Shells keep secrets, but I'm in the know,
They plot a coup against the tide's flow.
A fish swims by, gives a cheeky wink,
Before diving deep, makes me rethink.

So here I sit, my heart full of cheer,
In a comical dance with friends so near.
Life's a beach, with jokes less profound,
I'll ride the wave till I'm upside down!

Memories Carried on the Drift

A message in a bottle, what could it say?
Perhaps it's a drink order for the day.
A lonely rubber duck floats by with pride,
Waving hello, could it be my guide?

Sandcastles crumble like plans gone astray,
Tide comes in, washing dreams away.
But I find a flip-flop, a treasure to keep,
As I search for snacks and my shoes, too deep.

Driftwood tales, they twist and twine,
Like the tangled hair in my beachside shrine.
Shells shout stories, all funny and bold,
Of fish who tell tales and crabs who are told.

So gather 'round, let's share what we've found,
Like ice cream melting, it's messy, profound.
With laughter and joy, let the waves play their part,
As memories drift on, straight to the heart!

Dawn Breaks Over Solitude

A new day dawns with a sunny grin,
Pajamas and flip-flops, let the fun begin!
Coffee spills over my sandy throne,
As I chase seagulls, oh wait, they've flown.

Sunrise balloons bob in the air,
As I juggle my thoughts with crazy flair.
Do sunglasses make me look cool, or mad?
Maybe both, but it's all a bit rad!

Waves awaken with a frothy splash,
Seals bark loudly, as if to take cash.
I explain my dreams to a curious crab,
It nods along—what a listening fab!

So let the dawn roll, with its quirks and giggles,
I'll dance with shadows as the sunlight wiggles.
With laughter and bliss, the day starts anew,
In solitude's company, we'll laugh, me and you!

The Dance of Light on Water

Sunbeams shimmer with a cheeky sway,
Water twinkles like it wants to play.
Fishes flap to a beat all their own,
As I try to join in, using my phone.

Tidal pulls tug at my silly feet,
Trying to dance but just tasting the sea's heat.
A dolphin leaps with a sparkle and grin,
I envy its moves, wishing I could win!

Footprints in sand tell tales of the day,
Where laughter unraveled in whimsical fray.
Gulls steal my fries with the utmost delight,
While I throw confetti—oh, what a sight!

So let the light dance, let the ripples tease,
With each little wave, it's a laugh and a breeze.
Together we sway, me and the sea,
In this silly jig, we're forever carefree!

Ebbing Thoughts Beneath the Stars

At twilight's call, I trip on sand,
A rogue wave greets, oh what a hand!
I chase my dreams, they run away,
Frolicking in waves, come back, I say!

The moon's reflection starts to dance,
A jellyfish takes my pants by chance!
I laugh aloud, the sea's my friend,
With salty hugs that never end.

Starfish giggle, whispering low,
As crabs parade in quite a show.
I throw a shell, it spirals wide,
And watch it splash with goofy pride.

Beneath the dark, I spot a light,
A fading glow that brings me fright.
"Who needs a boat?" I shout with glee,
When seagulls laugh just like a spree!

Surrendered to the Gentle Sea

I lay prone on the soft, warm ground,
Expecting silence, birds abound.
A seagull lands, steals my snack,
And with a squawk, just turns his back!

The waves come giggling, what a sound,
Scooping seaweed all around.
They wrap me up in greenish glee,
A slimy hug, thank you, dear sea!

In every splash, a tickling plight,
I dive too deep, the fish take flight.
They dart with mirth as I emerge,
Bright faces gleam, like they'll converge.

The seashore's charm, so full of cheer,
With every swell, I'm glad I'm here.
I laugh and roll, a splendid mess,
In ocean's grasp, pure happiness!

Nature's Quiet Sanctuary

In quiet nooks, where twigs entwine,
I seek a spot where squirrels dine.
They wink at me from leafy high,
As I trip over roots nearby!

The breeze, a tease, it plays with hair,
I try to catch it, but it's rare.
The flowers blush with colors bright,
I sneeze—oh no! What a sight!

Crickets chirp, a concert great,
While toads perform, and I debate.
Should I join in, or just observe,
These nature stars with real good verve?

But as I sway to nature's tune,
A sudden splash! They greet the moon.
In this wild spot, I laugh and play,
In nature's arms, I drift away!

Shimmering Refuges by the Water's Edge

The rivers shimmer, tickling toes,
As I proceed, the mud just flows.
With every step, I lose my grace,
A splash erupts, the fish embrace!

Paddle boats float past with flair,
Each captain looks with sunscreen glare.
They wave with joy, I wave with muck,
Oh boaters, please send me some luck!

A crab scuttles, with quite a plan,
It's got my flip-flop; what a scam!
I tumble back to claim my prize,
While turtles chat with keen surprise.

With laughter bubbling, the sun dips low,
As colors blend in a gentle glow.
I raise my arms, let joy ignite,
In nature's arms, everything's right!

Harmonies of the Wind and Sea

Waves giggle as they frolic high,
Seagulls squawk as if they can fly.
A crab dances, his moves quite bold,
While clams are gossiping, secrets told.

The sun sneezes, then hides behind clouds,
As beach balls bounce and laughter shrouds.
Shells are busy, playing peek-a-boo,
And even the tide seems to have a clue.

Flip-flops chatter as they hit the sand,
Warm breezes blow, oh isn't it grand?
Picnics spread with jelly and jam,
While kids try to catch an elusive clam.

The ocean's jokes flow with every wave,
As surfboards wobble, they misbehave.
In this mirthful dance with foam and spray,
Life's a beach—come laugh along and play!

Where the Sky Kisses the Ocean

Ducks rowdy, play tag with the sun,
While mermaids giggle, having their fun.
Clouds are waiting, all fluffy and bright,
Playing peek-a-boo through the daylight.

A surfboard sails, like a bird on a spree,
While fish in the surf flash their glee.
Kites soar high, like balloons in the air,
As the breeze whispers, 'Adventure is rare!'

The sand's a canvas for doodles and art,
Where laughter and smiles pull at the heart.
Seashells chime in a jokester's choir,
As the tide keeps dancing, never to tire.

With every splash, a new comic scene,
The sun sets low, casting gold in between.
Laughter lingers as the day drifts by,
At this blissful spot, oh me, oh my!

Reflections on a Peaceful Tide

Mirror-like waters hold a silly grin,
As fish make faces, wearing a fin.
Little boats bob like they're in a dance,
While the sun takes a moment for a sunbathing trance.

Waves whisper secrets to sandy shores,
While jellybeans are hiding within their cores.
Crabby folks grumble, 'Where's the ice cream?'
But even the tide joins in on the dream.

The sun wears shades, all cool and bright,
As beach towels spread, in the golden light.
Kids are digging for treasure in sand,
Broad grins and laughter, oh isn't it grand?

With each playful splash, troubles disband,
In this joyous world crafted by hand.
Relaxation reigns, but fun's not far,
On this lively tide under the sun's radar!

Starlit Nights and Gentle Tides

Moonbeams giggle, dance on the waves,
As shadows play tricks in the lanterns' graves.
The ocean breathes softly, a lullaby sweet,
While flip-flops rest, tired from their feet.

Starfish hold court with stories to share,
As crickets serenade, without a care.
Gentle tides tease, pulling shells too near,
With a wink, they say, 'Don't bring your fear!'

Marshmallow clouds drift close for a chat,
About a sea turtle who once wore a hat.
Laughing waves beckon, 'Join in the play!'
Under the stars, let worries decay.

Bonfire sparks dance in the cool night air,
Smores roasting slowly—oh, do we dare!
With laughter echoing, the night is alive,
As we drift into dreams where giggles thrive!

Threads of Silken Ocean Light

A seagull steals my sandwich slice,
Flaunting its aerial heist so nice.
I chase it down the sandy trail,
While laughing at my lunchtime fail.

The waves giggle at my plight,
As I trip over my flip-flop's might.
A crab scuttles with a sassy wave,
Reminding me, I'm not so brave.

I find a shell that sings a tune,
It's off-key - sounds just like a loon.
I dance with seaweed on my head,
In this funny life, I'm never dread.

Ebb and flow in a silly chase,
The ocean laughs, and I embrace.
With every splash and tumble down,
I'm crowned the jester of this town.

Poetry of the Rippled Surface

The waves compose a quirky rhyme,
As I sip lemonade, feeling sublime.
A fish jumps high, flops down with grace,
Splashing water all over my face.

The sun winks at my soaked attire,
While clouds conspire, plotting to tire.
I try to keep my picnic afloat,
But seagulls' laughter is hard to quote.

An octopus tangled in a straw,
Squirts me with joy – it's not against the law!
With each little wave and bubbly cheer,
I know the ocean's humor is near.

A turtle rolls by with a frown,
He's in no rush; he's been around town.
I join in his slow-motion dance,
Finding laughter in every chance.

Chasing Serenity Across the Bay

I set my sail, but the wind goes astray,
Dragging my boat in a futile ballet.
The dolphins tease as they twirl and spin,
While I'm flapping about like a confused twin.

On my paddleboard, I look quite absurd,
Clashing with seagulls, feeling disturbed.
I shout, 'Catch me if you can!', what a ruckus,
They dive and dart, the sneaky ruckus!

The sunbeams laugh at my water ballet,
As I flail like a fish – what's my foray?
But as I tumble, I learn with ease,
Joy hides where it breezes with a tease.

Every splash is a song, every dip is delight,
As I dance with the tide, it feels so right.
Chasing the calm can be quite the game,
In this wacky world, nothing feels the same.

Silhouettes in Sunset Glow

The sun dips low, casting shadows bold,
A crab's in a hurry; it's quite a hold!
I trip on my beach towel, down I go,
The only witness is a seagull's crow.

Sandcastles rise like dreams of the day,
But watch out! Here comes a rogue wave - hooray!
It crashes down, my fortress is toast,
Now I'm left with a humorous ghost.

A pair of flamingos waltz in the mist,
Strutting their stuff, they can't be dismissed.
While I, in a ballet of awkward moves,
Turn the beach party into my own grooves.

As twilight blends in with giggles and tides,
I bask in the fun where laughter abides.
With silhouettes fading, the stars come alive,
And in this embrace, my spirit will thrive.

The Language of Gentle Waves

Waves giggle like children at play,
Splashing around in a joyful display.
They whisper secrets, oh so sly,
While seagulls cackle and swoop by.

Bubbles burst with a pop and a cheer,
Joking with fish who swim near.
They dance on the foam, what a sight,
Who knew that the ocean's so polite?

The tides have a rhythm, a quirky beat,
With crabs doing the cha-cha, oh, what a treat!
A conch shell laughs, it surely must know,
That life on the shore has a certain glow.

So gather 'round with a smile so wide,
You'll hear the waves sing, with joy as your guide.
They've got punchlines and puns in their flow,
Who knew the sea could put on a show?

Calm Reflections on a Glassy Sea

Mirror, mirror, on the bay's floor,
Do you hold jokes behind your calm door?
A fish flashes a grin, oh so sly,
As reflections send ripples, and the seagulls fly.

Waves in their silence do giggle and gleam,
In this glassy expanse, life's but a dream.
A sea turtle glides like a connoisseur,
While kelp tickles the fish, oh so demure.

Look at those shells, what stories they tell,
Of beachside parties and seaweed spells.
The starfish strikes a pose, chic and grand,
In the water's reflection, humor is planned.

So take a seat on this tranquil shore,
Let giggles of waves be the night's score.
For laughter lingers where peace seems to dwell,
In reflections that sparkle like a shimmering bell.

Twilight's Embrace on the Water

As dusk approaches, colors collide,
The sea laughs aloud, full of pride.
The sun takes a bow, what a grand show,
While dolphins joke about what they know.

Silver fish flash like wild disco lights,
As crabs take the stage for their salsa nights.
Turtles don shades, feeling quite hip,
While starfish spin tales, giving the flip.

With twilight's glow, the sea starts to wink,
While boats bobbing laugh, offering a drink.
A clam with a grin yells, "I'm pearl of the day!"
Who knew that twilight could make waves play?

So let the night wrap its arms around,
With laughter and joy, let peace abound.
For in twilight's embrace, every heart is free,
In this frolicking realm, come join the spree!

Whispers of the Aquatic Realm

Underwater gossip, oh, what a tease,
Coral reefs chuckle in a gentle breeze.
What's that bubble? A rumor gone wild,
The octopus grins, he's so well-styled.

Eels with their antics swim through the fun,
While jellyfish float, just basking in sun.
A clownfish jokes, "Life's never a bore!"
The seaweed sways, joining the score.

Ripples of laughter roll over the sand,
As shells share secrets, perfectly planned.
A crab says, "Look, I've got moves so fine!"
And the ocean joins in, singing, "You're divine!"

So dive into laughter, let joy reign supreme,
In this aquatic world, life's an endless dream.
For the whispers of water carry glee,
A sea full of smiles, come ride the spree!

Blue Waters

The waves are blue and so am I,
Splashed by fish that swim on by.
A crab's sharp pinch gave me a fright,
I danced away in pure delight.

Seagulls squawk and steal my fries,
As I gaze up at cloudy skies.
With sunscreen drenched on my nose,
I'm the latest beachside pose!

A family's picnic turns to war,
When ants come marching, seeking more.
Sandcastles crumble, oh what a sight,
While a sandman sneezes, what a night!

The sun sets low, my skin's all red,
Guess I should have stayed in bed.
Yet laughing waves will always call,
For I'm the clown of beachside hall!

Quiet Thoughts

Finding peace beneath the sun,
While seagulls dive, oh what fun!
Turtles surf on seashell boards,
As I ponder scores of hoards.

Thoughts of jelly, splish, and splash,
Made of giggles, oh what a clash!
Sand in my sandwich, quite bizarre,
But the taste? It's a total star!

As I daydream of fish in pants,
My mind wanders to silly chants.
What if crabs have secret cues?
Dancing sideways in beachy blues!

With every wave, my cares all fade,
But the thought of sandcastles made.
Turns out they topple with great flair,
And I am left, doing my hair!

Echoes of the Distant Lighthouse

Far away, a light does gleam,
I wonder if it's just a dream.
A pirate ship with silly hats,
Sails by in search of candy cats!

Echoes bounce like bouncing balls,
As dolphins throw their playful calls.
Whales below, they sing a tune,
While I'm here inventing balloons!

A lighthouse keeper, lost in thought,
Counts seagulls, doubles every shot.
His beard is long, a nest of snacks,
Popcorn and gumdrops fill the cracks!

As night falls down, the spotlight sways,
My beachside laughter rings for days.
With every echo, giggles bloom,
In this sea of chaotic room!

Moonlit Paths on Silken Sands

Moonlight dances on the tide,
While I clumsily glide and slide.
Footprints vanish, sand so fine,
My pizza cravings? Quite divine!

Stars twinkle like holiday lights,
As crabs in tuxedos have their fights.
A mermaid offers me a snack,
But I just want my nacho stack!

Sea turtles snicker, rolling by,
In tuxedos, oh my oh my!
They laugh as I trip on my shoe,
Splashing moonlight - here's my cue!

But with each step, I feel so grand,
Despite the mishaps on this land.
Under the glow, my worries drown,
As moonbeams gift me an evening crown!

Serenity Amongst the Coral Reefs

Coral castles hide fish in crowns,
While I float 'round with silly frowns.
A grouper grins, it's quite absurd,
Telling me all the latest word!

Underwater giggles speed and dart,
As clownfish dance, they steal my heart.
"Why so serious?" one fish remarked,
"Join the party!" as he sparkled and sparked!

Octopuses juggle seashells with flair,
While sea horses twirl in midair.
Together the reef sings a tune,
That tickles my toes like a sunny balloon!

In this vibrant, wacky retreat,
I surrender to nature's beat.
As bubbles float, my joy sets sail,
On this coral reef, I can't fail!

Driftwood Dreams at Twilight

A stick floats by on the tide's soft sway,
It thinks it's a boat, oh what a play!
Seagulls joke, they squawk with delight,
As driftwood dreams dance in the night.

A crab joins in with a shuffle and slide,
He's got no boat, yet takes it in stride.
With a wink and a wave, he scuttles along,
Under the moon, the twilight sings a song.

They gather for laughter on sandy lanes,
Trading old tales, forgetting their pains.
As sea foam tickles and splashes their feet,
The driftwood and crab make the night complete.

Oh, if only logs could laugh like we do,
They'd join in the chuckles from me and you!
In the ocean's vast jest, they float and they bob,
Creating a scene that would make any mob!

Serene Horizons Unfurled

A turtle wearing sunglasses takes a stroll,
Waves crashing, he giggles, life's a funny role.
He stops for a snack, munching on seaweed,
With humor and smiles, he exceeds the need.

The sun winks down, a mischievous ray,
As crabs do the cha-cha, having their say.
Dolphins dive near, playing peek-a-boo,
In this comedy show, it's all brand new.

A flip-flop floats by, lost in the tide,
Whispers of laughter, the ocean's pride.
Children giggle as they splash all around,
With joy painted bright, and silliness found.

As horizons extend, and stories unfold,
The laughter of nature, pure joy to behold.
A party of waves, with their frothy cheer,
In this funny world, there's nothing to fear.

Calm Currents of the Heart

Fish don top hats, and wriggle with grace,
In this tranquil water, there's no need to race.
A lobster's a dancer, debuting tonight,
In a seashell theater, oh what a sight!

Now a clownfish arrives, sporting big shoes,
Says "Let's have a party, we've got nothing to lose!"
He juggles the sandcastles, proud of his act,
While seaweed sways, keeping the rhythm intact.

The gentle waves giggle, tickling the bay,
As the tide plays its tune, it sways and it sways.
A starfish does splits, oh what will he do?
With the currents of laughter, his worries are few.

Amongst all the silliness, the heart finds its beat,
In the calm of the ocean, where joy is complete.
So come join the laughter, let your spirit take flight,
In this whimsical world, where everything's bright!

Sandcastles of Solitude

A plucky grain of sand dreams big of a tower,
While hermit crabs giggle, embracing their power.
They build with a flourish, each goof a delight,
As wind plays a trick, in the soft starlit night.

A seagull swoops down, all dramatic and grand,
As the castle tumbles, it's all part of the plan.
"Don't fret!", chirps the sand, "It's just a quick fall!"
With laughter, they rebuild, their spirits stand tall.

As tides roll in and out, a rhythm so sweet,
The mishaps of nature make everything neat.
With buckets and laughter, they all shout with glee,
Building sandcastles of dreams, just you wait and see!

In solitude's embrace, friends find what is true,
With sand in their toes and skies oh so blue.
Under the glow, they craft what's absurd,
A kingdom of smiles, where dreams are deferred.

Footprints on the Quiet Sand

A crab scuttled by in a tiny race,
Leaving footprints all over the place.
I tried to follow, but fell in the bay,
Now my shoes are soggy, what more can I say?

The seagulls squawked, doing a jig,
While I performed a triumphant wig.
They stole my sandwich, I just can't compete,
But watching them dance? Now that's a treat!

We built a sandcastle, ten feet tall,
Only to see it collapse with a fall.
A beach bum laughed and tossed me a shell,
Saying, "Watch for waves, your dress could tell!"

So here I stand, with a laugh and a grin,
On this sandy stage where giggles begin.
With each silly stumble and funny mess,
I find life's joy, I must confess!

Celestial Conversations by the Water

Stars were debating about who shines best,
While I sipped coconut and laughed with zest.
The moon chimed in, 'I'm large and I glow!'
The sun just chuckled, 'That's all just for show!'

A dolphin pod floated, sharing their tunes,
Singing of fish and bright silver moons.
I joined in, off-key, but full of delight,
'They must be impressed, I'm a star in this night!'

Crabs joined the chat, each with a quirk,
Claiming to have the best footwork at work.
But when they danced, it was clumsy and strange,
Leaving us rolling with laughter, quite deranged!

As waves whispered secrets, the stars gave a cheer,
In the water's reflection, friends gathered near.
With laughter and magic in this joyful spree,
The cosmos feels light, and I'm part of the glee!

Portraits of Ocean's Embrace

The ocean posed like a cheeky uncle,
With waves that giggle and bubbles that crinkle.
Caught in the moment, I took a brave shot,
But my hair flew wild—an artistic mishap!

A fish swam by, donned in some bling,
Its scales were shining, a true ocean king.
I asked for a selfie, it swished with a blink,
And with a splashy farewell, it made me rethink!

A beach ball rolled in, all covered in sand,
Bouncing around, just as it planned.
It stopped for a moment, gave a comical spin,
And left me tossing, just trying to grin!

With laughter as colors and footprints like art,
The canvas of beachfront stole every heart.
In this humorous realm by the shimmering sea,
I'm capturing memories, just being me!

Gentle Horizons at Dusk

As the sun dipped low and the sky turned pink,
I half-heartedly tried to balance and blink.
Waves tickled my toes, they whispered and swayed,
While I tripped over driftwood, again I displayed!

A pelican strutted, all pomp and all flair,
While I made my best bird-face with wind in my hair.
It tilted its head, as if to assess,
And then it just squawked, I felt such a mess!

The horizon grinned, playing tricks with the light,
Each color a joke in this glorious sight.
I laughed with the clouds, dancing high on a breeze,
As they transformed into shapes— oh, what a tease!

So here's to the evening, the giggles we share,
With each silly moment, we lighten the air.
In twilight's embrace, we find laughter's tune,
Let's dance with the dusk, beneath the bright moon!

Echoes in the Dunes

There once was a crab, quite a fan,
Dancing in sand, like a little man.
A seagull swooped down, made a funny face,
The crab just laughed, what a silly race!

A beach ball rolled in, all tangled in seaweed,
The crab tried to kick it, oh what a need!
But he tripped on a shell, went tumbling around,
While giggling and clapping, he fell on the ground.

Turtles watched, munching on lunch so divine,
As the crab told his tales, it was truly a sign.
"Life's like the tides, always making you sway,
Just add a good laugh, and you'll brighten the day!"

In the end, they all joined in a silly parade,
With shells as their hats, none were afraid.
On the shores of their laughter, they found a great spell,
Echoes of joy in the seashells they fell.

Meadow of the Twilight Breeze

In the twilight, bees buzzed with flair,
While rabbits in bow ties danced without care.
A hedgehog rolled by with a leap and a twirl,
Spinning and smiling like a little pearl.

The flowers all giggled, petals in bloom,
As a fox tried to waltz, creating a room.
With moonlight above and a starry display,
They twirled 'round the meadow, watch them sway!

An owl with a monocle offered some wisdom,
Told a joke about bees, it caused quite a rhythm.
The laughter erupted, wild and free,
In a meadow of twilight, as fun as can be!

When the sun dipped low, they called it a night,
With a hat made of grass, such a hilarious sight.
They gathered their treasures, each giggle a spark,
In their joyful garden, they left their sweet mark.

Secrets of the Salted Air

A pelican landed with flair on a pier,
He stumbled right over; his fish went in fear.
With a flap and a flap, he tried to take flight,
But he missed the horizon and landed in fright.

Seagulls were chatting, plotting some fun,
They quacked and they squawked beneath the sun.
They dove for some fries left behind on a plate,
While the pelican grumbled, "Such tempting fate!"

A dolphin swam by, with a wink and a tease,
"Join us, my friend, we'll make quite a spree!"
A splash and a flip, the pelican joined,
Soon everyone knew; his grace had been coined.

As waves swept in, they danced in such style,
Their laughter erupted, stretching a mile.
In secrets of salted air, they found a way,
To turn every blunder into a fine day!

Kaleidoscope of Serene Moments

In a garden where laughter bloomed like a rose,
A couple of frogs put on colorful clothes.
With a hop and a skip, they leaped to the beat,
Spinning and twirling in footwear so neat.

Butterflies chuckled, swirling nearby,
While ants marched on, looking spry as they fly.
The frogs flipped their hats with glee and delight,
Jumping like stars in their own constellation night.

A sly little fox, with tricks up his sleeve,
Told puns to the crowd, who couldn't believe.
With a ribbit, a giggle, they formed quite a show,
In a kaleidoscope charm, they let laughter grow.

As the sun gently dipped below the wide trees,
The garden grew quiet, still buzzing with ease.
Every moment of joy, every shared quip,
Made memories swirl like a joyous road trip.

Reverie of a Moonlit Bay

Beneath the moon, a fish wears shades,
A crab learns salsa on sandy parades.
Dolphins are giggling, waving their tails,
While seagulls gossip about fishy trails.

The tide rolls in with a frothy laugh,
Shells play poker, each one a half.
A starfish shouts, "I want to be free!"
While octopuses juggle, as funny as can be.

Whales do cartwheels, making a splash,
And sandcastles topple in a dandy crash.
The beach chair's dancing, it's quite a sight,
As flip-flops twirl in the moonlit night.

As laughter bounces from wave to wave,
Life's joyous dance is what we crave.
Beneath the stars, hilarity's hymn,
In this funny paradise, we dive right in.

Serenity in the Shell's Whisper

A clam named Fred tells jokes of old,
While seaweed rolls with laughter bold.
A starfish rolls its eyes in glee,
As jellyfish float, just carefree.

Crabs do a tango, legs all akimbo,
While fish recount tales of a great limbo.
Peering through shells, they listen to wit,
In a watery world, where humor's a hit.

Silvery shells sing a melody sweet,
As seagulls throw down some rhythmical beat.
The tide giggles soft, like secrets it keeps,
While the ocean snickers, as all nature leaps.

Bubbles float up with a chuckle so bright,
Each splash brings a grin in the warm moonlight.
In this shell-studded laughter, oh what a lore,
We find joy in the ocean, forevermore.

Canvas of Soft Seafoam

Painting the waves with giggles and cheer,
A dolphin's splashing, the coast is quite near.
Seashells in rows, snug in the sand,
As surfboards race on, quite out of hand.

A crab in a tutu, striking a pose,
With laughter erupting as the current flows.
The seafoam whispers secrets of grace,
While barnacles chuckle in their cozy space.

Kites dance above on a cheerful day,
With each gust of wind, they frolic and play.
The ocean's canvas, where fun never ends,
Painted in laughter, where humor transcends.

Waves weave their magic, a comedic embrace,
As we join the dance in this joyous place.
With wide-open minds, we gather 'neath sun,
In the soft seafoam haven, we all feel as one.

Driftwood Wishes

Driftwood whispers with a woodsy grin,
As sea turtles roll in their happy spin.
With treasures of laughter, the beach has its charm,
As seashells giggle, keeping us warm.

A pelican fumbles while trying to dine,
As seagulls chuckle, "Oh, what's your line?"
The surfboards are racing, not far from the shore,
While beach balls are bouncing, we can't help but roar.

With each wave that crashes, a song's softly sung,
Of flip-flops zipping like a kid that's just sprung.
The sand's got jokes, it tickles our toes,
While laughter erupts wherever it goes.

The moon shines down, a spotlight so bright,
Echoing joy in the cool, gentle night.
We gather our wishes on driftwood so wise,
In this funny paradise, laughter never dies.

Glimmers of Soft Light on Water

A sea otter floats with a grin,
Juggling seashells, where to begin?
The sun dances on waves, a playful show,
While a crab in a tuxedo puts on a row.

Seagulls squawk in a karaoke spree,
Singing about fish and the great briny sea.
With flip-flops aplenty, we scamper and slide,
Chasing sea breeze with laughter as our guide.

A mermaid's stuck in a fishing net,
Yelling for help with no signs of regret.
Her scales glimmer bright in the daylight's embrace,
While starfish join in, trying to keep pace.

Sandy toes inherit the tide's joyful song,
As kids build castles that never last long.
Yet each wave that crashes just makes us believe,
That giggles and bubbles are what we receive.

Emotions Carried by the Tide

The tide rolls in, with a wink and a nudge,
Sandcastles teeter; we give them a grudge.
Surfers try to ride with the grace of a swan,
Instead, they crash down with a splash and a yawn.

A lobster wears glasses, feeling quite smart,
Reciting old poems, a true work of art.
The jellyfish jiggles, not one to be shy,
Waving hello as it floats softly by.

In a clam's little world, there's a dance party, too,
With conchs playing DJ, spinning tunes just for you.
While fish with big smiles wiggle and sway,
Forgetfulness reigns as they glide out to play.

But oh, when the waves toss their shimmering dreams,
We laugh with the sea, lost in happiness streams.
With laughter and bubbles, the shore serves its pride,
As the tide carries joy with each playful ride.

Bliss Found in Still Waters

A duck wearing boots steps out for a stroll,
On a pond that's so still, it could swallow a whole.
With ripples for friends, they giggle and cheer,
While lily pads listen to all that they hear.

The frogs start to croak like a band on the rise,
Pondering the secrets of the starry skies.
Their croaks form a symphony, quirky and loud,
As starlight spills laughs like it's part of the crowd.

Paddling around, a squirrel takes a dive,
Re-emerging drenched, just too glad to survive.
With twirls made of feathers, a swan takes the stage,
While the turtles roll back, gossiping from their cage.

In still waters, joy ripples out like a spree,
Where every critter is simply carefree.
Each moment is funny, with smiles to bestow,
On the dance floor of dreams, where giggles just flow.

Shadows of Clouds on Serene Seas

A cloud whispered secrets to a wave far below,
'Do you think dolphins catch wind of our show?'
The wave laughed and shimmered, all frothy and bright,
While the clouds, like popcorn, drifted in flight.

An octopus paints with the colors it finds,
Each brushstroke a riddle, twisting and kind.
With jelly-young jellybeans, they party all day,
Laughing at sea monsters who dance in dismay.

Bizarre boaters parade in costumes bizarre,
Dressed as the cast of an old movie star.
Each time they pass by, they giggle and grin,
As the sun sets behind them, a little chagrin.

With shadows that swirled on the gentle tide's hum,
We watch as waves dance to the beat of a drum.
In the softness of twilight, the laughter nests sweet,
For in each funny moment, the heart finds its beat.

Embracing the Stillness of the Tide

A crab danced sideways, oh what a sight,
He thought he was quite the charming knight.
With a wink and a jig, he stole the show,
While seagulls laughed, putting on a row.

The ocean sighed, a soft, silly breeze,
As dolphins played tag with a splash and tease.
The sun wore shades like a beach-side fool,
Making waves of laughter, life's endless school.

A starfish claimed spots, the pride of the sand,
While jellyfish floated, as graceful as planned.
The tide tickled toes, a giggle or two,
As shells whispered secrets, just I and the blue.

Tranquility Wrapped in Seashells

In a shell, I found a tiny hat,
Worn by a snail who surely chats.
He offered me tea, a sip of the sea,
But I laughed so hard, I spilled on my knee.

With sand castles built, to the sky they climbed,
A fortress for crabs now perfectly primed.
They held a grand feast, with chips made of foam,
While the tide played DJ, calling it home.

The sun set down, painting skies all aglow,
As a fish told a joke about swimming too slow.
The waves rolled in laughter, rolling back out,
As shells held the echoes of giggles and shouts.

Whispers of Tranquil Waves

The waves had secrets, they softly shared,
With a clam who wore pearls, but no one cared.
He claimed he was royal, a quirky old brute,
Who swam with a crown and a mismatched suit.

A whale slid by, with a splash and a grin,
Telling tales of old ships and where they had been.
The clams rolled their eyes, a familiar sight,
As seaweed swayed like it was holding on tight.

The laugh of the gulls soared high in the sky,
While fish made a chorus, singing out why.
Each ripple a chuckle, a hug from the tide,
In this strange little world where silliness hides.

Echoes of Still Waters

On a rock sat a frog, with a top hat askew,
He croaked out a tune, quite off-key, yes it's true.
A turtle tapped toes, keeping up with the beat,
As minnows swam by, dancing light on their feet.

The pond splashed with giggles, a ball of delight,
While lily pads rolled like they were taking flight.
The echoing water held laughter galore,
As dragonflies swooped in for an encore.

A bubble arose, with a pop and a cheer,
While frogs joined hands, spreading joy far and near.
In this world of peace, where bliss is the game,
The echoes of fun will always remain.

www.ingramcontent.com/pod-product-compliance
Lightning Source LLC
Chambersburg PA
CBHW072131070526
44585CB00016B/1629